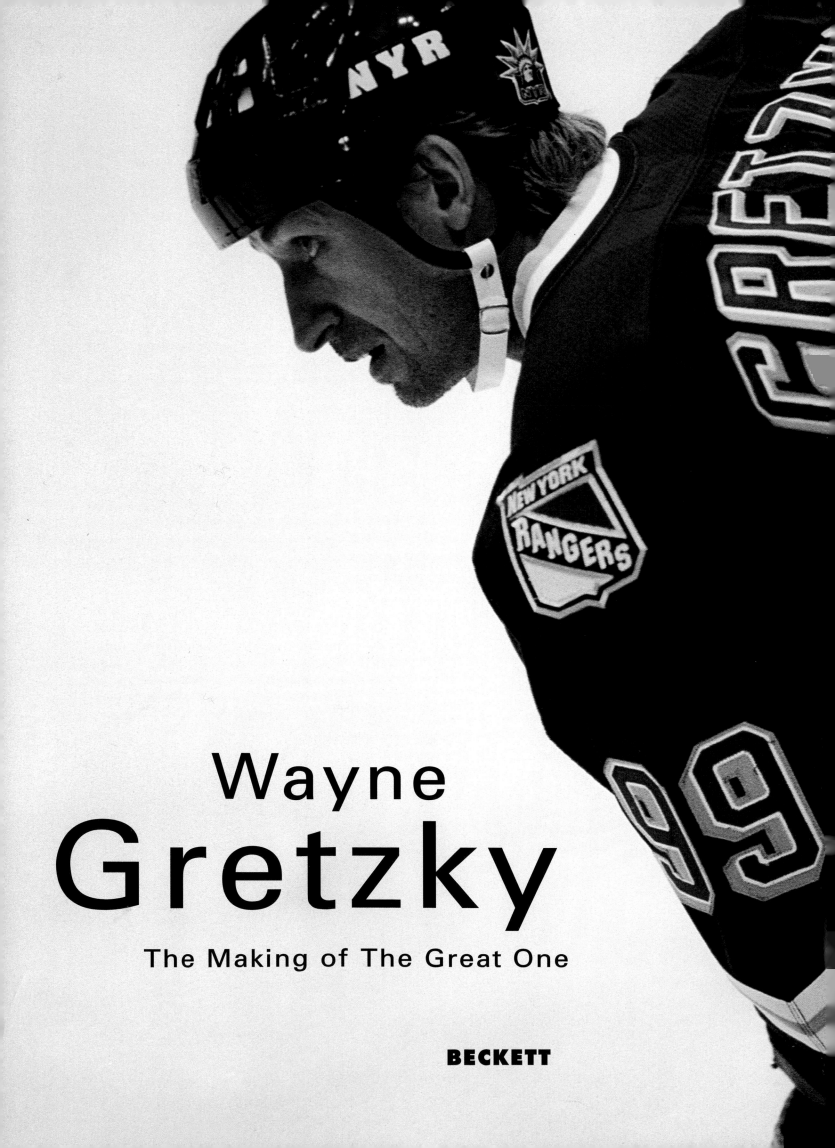

Wayne Gretzky

The Making of The Great One

BECKETT

Wayne Gretzky

The Making of The Great One

Copyright©1998
by Dr. James Beckett
All rights reserved under
International and
Pan-American Copyright
Conventions.

**Wayne Gretzky: The
Making of The Great One**
is not licensed, authorized
or endorsed by any
league, player or players
association, nor is it
authorized or endorsed by
Wayne Gretzky.

Published by:
Beckett Publications,
15850 Dallas Parkway,
Dallas, TX 75248

Manufactured in the
United States of America
ISBN: 1-887432-46-9

Cover photo by
Gary Moss / Outline

First Edition:
March 1998

CEO/Publisher Dr. James Beckett
President Jeff Amano
Vice President, Operations/Finance Claire B. Backus
Vice President & General Counsel Joe Galindo
Director, Distribution Beth Harwell
Director, Marketing Margaret Steele

Editorial
Group Publisher Rudy J. Klancnik
Managing Editor Tim Polzer
Senior Editor Steve Wilson
Assistant Editors Joel Brown, Aaron Derr
Staff Doug Williams (Photos); Eric Cash, Randy Cummings,
Tracy Hackler, Becky Hart, Douglas Kale, Justin Kanoya,
Mike McAllister, Al Muir, Mike Pagel, Mike Payne,
Jim Thompson, Mark Zeske

Art
Art Director Eric Evans
Senior Designer Jeff Stanton
Designer Tina Tackett
Staff Judi Smalling (Artwork); Therese Bellar,
Amy Brougher, Bob Johnson, Sara Leeman,
Sara Maneval, Missy Patton, Lisa Runyon,
Len Shelton, Roz Theesfeld

Sports Data Publishing Pepper Hastings (Group Publisher),
Dan Hitt (Manager), Mark Anderson, Pat Blandford,
Theo Chen, Jeany Finch, Michael Jaspersen, Steven Judd,
Rich Klein, Lon Levitan, Beverly Mills, Gabriel Rangel,
Grant Sandground, Rob Springs, Bill Sutherland

Prepress Randall Calvert, (Manager), Pete Adauto,
Belinda Cross, Marlon DePaula, Ryan Duckworth,
Maria L. Gonzalez-Davis, Paul Kerutis, Lori Lindsey,
Daniel Moscoso, Clark Palomino, Andrea Paul,
Susan Sainz

Advertising Sales Jeff Anthony (Director),
Matt McGuire, Mike Obert, Dave Sliepka; Shawn Murphy
(Media Research); Lauren Drewes (Intern)

Advertising Inquiries (972) 448-4600
Fax (972) 233-6488

Dealer Advertising Craig Ferris (Manager), Louise Bird,
Bridget Norris, Don Pendergraft, Phaedra Strecher,
Ed Wornson, David Yandry (972) 448-9168

Dealer Account & General Information (972) 991-6657

Subscription calls only (800) 840-3137

Book Sales Kevin King

Direct Sales Bob Richardson (Manager), Julie Binion,
Marty Click, Wendy Pallugna, Brett Setter

Corporate Sales Patti Harris (Manager), Angie Calandro,
Kandace Elmore, Jeff Greer, Joanna Hayden,
Laura Patterson, Sheri Smith, Marcia Stoesz

Marketing Mike Gullatt (Manager), Mary Campana,
Von Daniel, Robert Gregory, Gayle Klancnik, Hugh Murphy,
Dawn Sturgeon

New Media Omar Mediano (Manager), Cara Carmichael,
Amy Durrett, Tom Layberger, John Marshall, Jay Zwerner

Subscriptions Margie Swoyer (Manager),
Jenifer Grellhesel, Christine Seibert

Information Services Airey Baringer (Senior Manager),
Dana Alecknavage, Chris Hellem

Distribution Randy Mosty (Manager), Albert Chavez,
Daniel Derrick, Gean Paul Figari, Mark Hartley,
Ben Leme, Blake Timme, Bryan Winstead

Facilities Jim Tereschuk (Manager), Bob Brown

Accounting Teri McGahey (Manager), Susan Catka,
Mitchell Dyson, Sherry Monday

Operations Mary Gregory (Manager), Kaye Ball,
Loretta Gibbs, Rosanna Gonzalez-Oleachea, Julie Grove,
Stanley Lira, Mila Morante, Stacy Olivieri, Doree Tate

Human Resources Jane Ann Layton (Manager),
Carol Fowler

Dealer Accounts Correspondence All correspondence
regarding consignment sales of Beckett Products should
be addressed to: Dealer Accounts, 15850 Dallas Parkway,
Dallas, Texas 75248.

World Wide Web Home Page http://www.beckett.com

Skatearound

BY GORDIE HOWE

Right from the start, I noticed Wayne was different from other young hockey players.

The first time I met Wayne was at an awards banquet in Brantford, Ontario (when Wayne was 11). I remember it very well. Now, I had been doing these type of awards dinners for more than 25 years, but this one was a little different. What made it so was Wayne. There was just something about him even then that made him stand out. He was more mature, more aware of things. I could tell by the way he handled himself around other people.

What immediately struck me about him was the fact he asked so many questions — and the type of questions he asked. He didn't ask about the National Hockey League, or necessarily how to get there. He asked me questions about how to improve: what I did to improve, what sort of things I worked on and how I practiced those things.

That really struck me. Here's a young kid scoring all these goals (378 in the 1971-72 season), and he was asking me how to improve his backhand and, in general, all his shots. He was eager to

improve, and that's the mark of any truly great player. Wayne is certainly that.

I knew it wouldn't take long for Wayne to break my records. As long as he stayed healthy, that was the key. I'm happy that if anyone were to break my records in this game, it would be Wayne. He's such a great ambassador for hockey that he always has time for fans and the media. He only does what's best for the game.

Wayne Gretzky broke Gordie Howe's legendary NHL records of 1,850 career points and 801 goals in 1989 and '94, respectively. But The Great One contends the record book is the only place he ranks above his idol, Mr. Hockey. "There's one Gordie Howe," No. 99 says of No. 9. "That's all there is to that."

Ted Kulfan, who interviewed Gordie Howe for this story, covers professional hockey for The Detroit News.

Contents

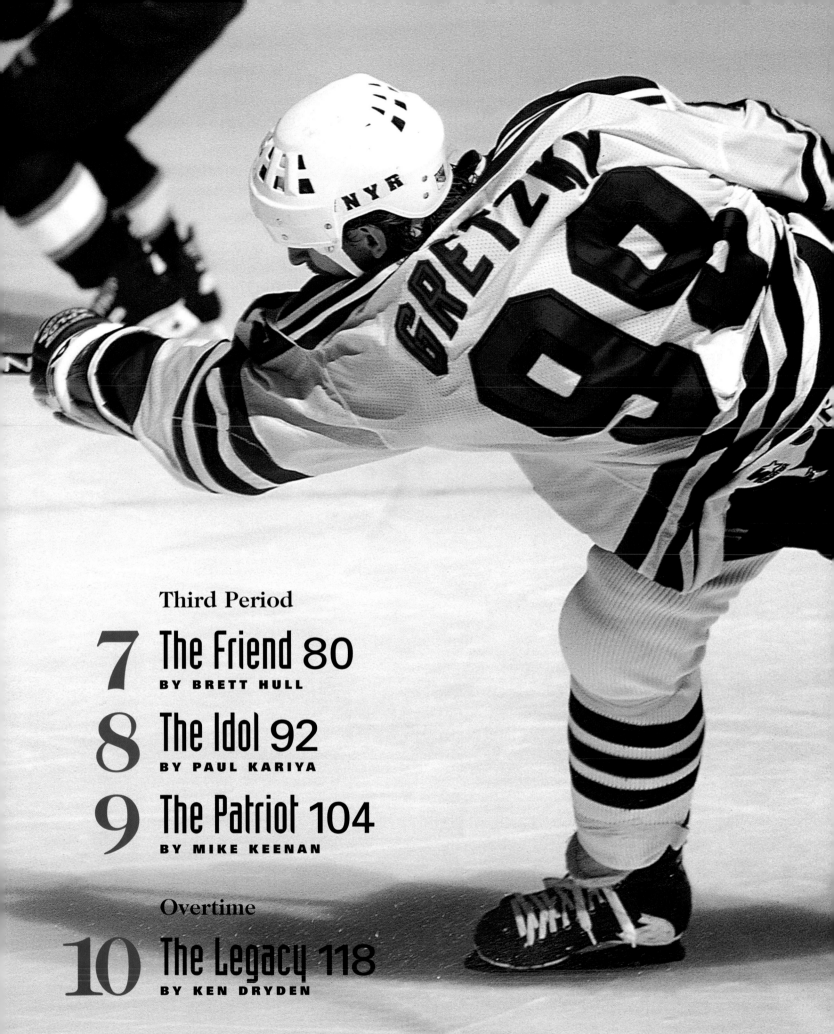

First Period

The Great One

If you watch Wayne Gretzky, and he just steps out on the ice and you watch him practice, a lot of times you will not notice him. He is not gifted physically like other players. He doesn't have Mario Lemieux's great size and reach and Jaromir Jagr's great size and reach and skating ability. He doesn't have Eric Lindros' strength or that type of thing — or Bobby Hull's great shot. It is just whenever that puck touches him, and whenever the game starts, he just changes. He is the best player in the world. I don't think there will ever be another one like him. He just sees the ice. The plays he makes, the thinking he does, is so far ahead of anyone I have ever seen, played for or watched.

BY BARRY MELROSE

"They come along

very, very seldom.

Basketball has one in

(Michael) Jordan,

and we have one

in Wayne."

article where they picked the best of everything, I think he was only in one category.

And here is a guy who scored 92 goals when no one has ever come close, and he is not classified as a goal scorer.

It is hilarious when I look at this and see what he has done, and that is what makes him special. What do you say about him? With Mario, you can say, "greatest stick handler ever." With Bobby Hull you can say, "the hardest shot ever." With Gordie Howe you can say, "the consummate professional who does everything."

But with Wayne, it's different.

He is the greatest passer without a doubt. He sees the ice better than anyone. He can lay a saucer pass over three sticks and put it on Jari Kurri's stick for a one-timer. He will see a defenseman coming down the middle of the rink from the far blue line that no one else can see.

He is not the best at everything, but he is the best who has ever played. I use the word "unique" because there is no one else like him. Every night he does something that just shocks me.

I think Bobby Orr changed the game, and if he would have stayed healthy, his numbers would have been phenomenal. Like Gretzky, Orr loved the game, Orr always spoke well, Orr had an aura around him and Orr sold the game night in and night out wherever he was. I think Orr is the closest. Mario is an

immense talent, but for the whole package, the two guys are Orr and Gretzky.

I always laugh at the old-timers who say, "The original six . . . don't forget the original six." The biggest players (when the NHL was a six-team league) were 6 feet tall and 170 pounds. Wayne Gretzky is doing these things against 6-4, 230-pound guys. He is doing it with players from all over the world.

My favorite Gretzky story would probably be the 1993 Stanley Cup semifinals (when the Kings rallied to defeat the Toronto Maple Leafs in seven brutal games).

We were down, and Toronto had the great defense, and people said Gretzky wasn't going to be able to score, and we did not stand a chance. But he played two great games: in Game 6, when he scored in overtime, and Game 7, when he scored a hat trick. The bigger the game, the bigger he plays. It is a great indication of what he is.

From **Edmonton** to **L.A.** to St. **Louis** to **New York**, Gretzky has **relished** the role of **hockey's** ambassador.

He is different than 99 percent of the athletes in today's game. He is such an ambassador of the sport, and he loves the sport. He loves to sell the sport, and it is not work for him to say good things about hockey. It is not work for him to make himself available for interviews. It is not work for him to do the things that are work for other players, and I think that comes across when you interview him. He loves the game.

I have always said of all the superstars in the world, I was lucky to coach the best one.

When it comes to speaking with authority on hockey, there are few people in and around the NHL who can compete with Barry Melrose.

That's because Melrose has done anything and everything in hockey.

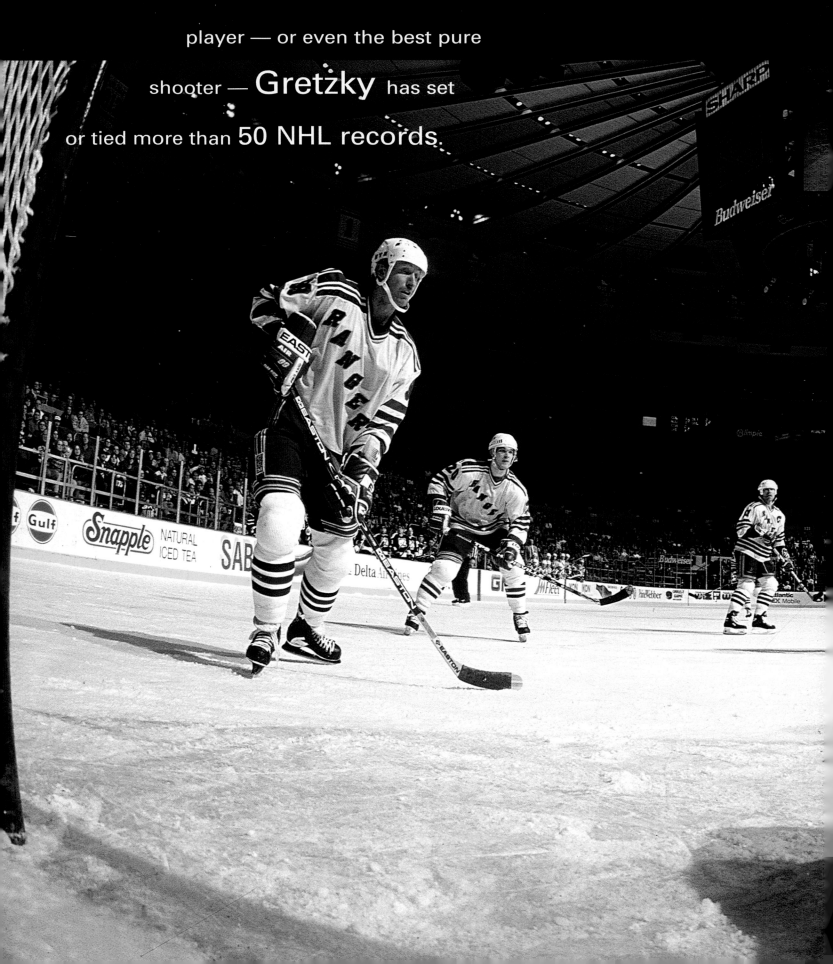

Not **considered** by many

to be the **strongest** or fastest

player — or even the best pure

shooter — **Gretzky** has set

or tied more than **50 NHL records**.

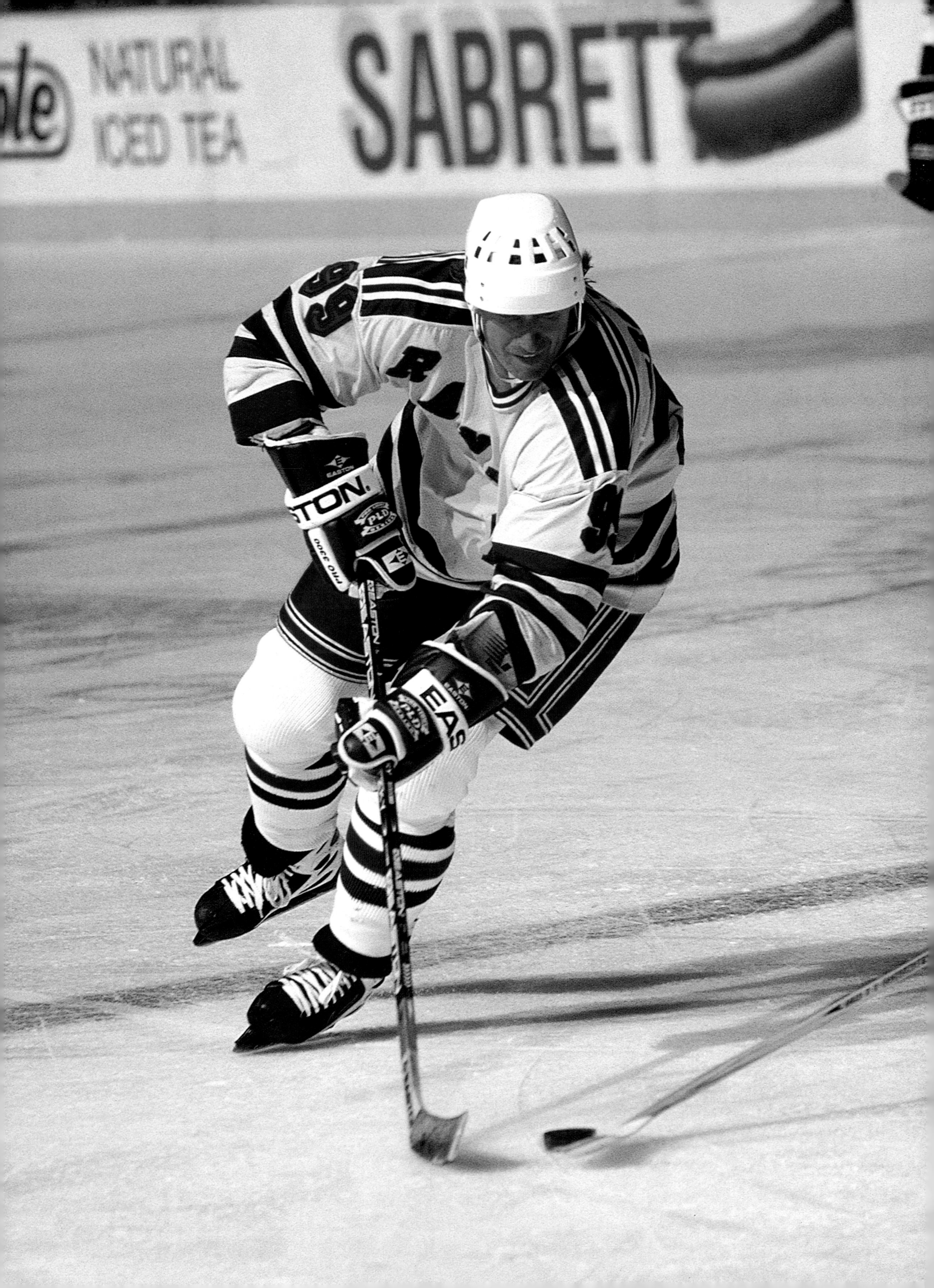
NATURAL
ICED TEA
SABRETT
EASTON
EASTON

His media credits include working as a studio analyst for National Hockey Night on ESPN and ESPN2's NHL 2Night. He also has worked select games on ESPN2, provided reports for SportsCenter and contributed to ESPN Radio regularly during the season.

After serving as a defenseman who played 335 games with Winnipeg, Toronto and Detroit from 1979 to 1986, Melrose began his coaching career in 1987 in Medicine Hat, Alberta. He then made the jump to the pro leagues and joined the Adirondack Red Wings of the American Hockey League in 1989. His team won the Calder Cup in 1991.

"He will do things in a **game** nobody else **can** or has ever tried."

In 1992, Melrose was hired as head coach of the Los Angeles Kings, where he and Wayne Gretzky developed a long-lasting friendship. With Gretzky helping to lead the way, Melrose's knack of taking his team to the finals continued. Under Melrose's watch, the Kings advanced to the Stanley Cup finals for the first time in franchise history in '92-93 before falling to the Montreal Canadiens.

Alan Adams, who interviewed Barry Melrose for this story, covers the NHL for the Toronto Star.

GRETZKY

99

2

BY GRANT FUHR

I saw him play before I ever met him.
Growing up in Edmonton, I got a
chance to see him with the Oilers in the
World Hockey Association. All the
papers were saying that he was just a
little skinny kid out there. But you could
see he could play. You just didn't realize how good he is until you played with
him every day. What impressed me the
first time I saw him was that he sees the
ice so well. I think he sees the ice better
than anybody else. That's one of his
biggest keys. He just reads the game so
much better. Plays that other people
don't see, he sees. He reads where
other people are going to be. People

The Scorer

Gretzky's masterful blend of grace and speed revolutionized a game once dominated by brute force and sheer power.

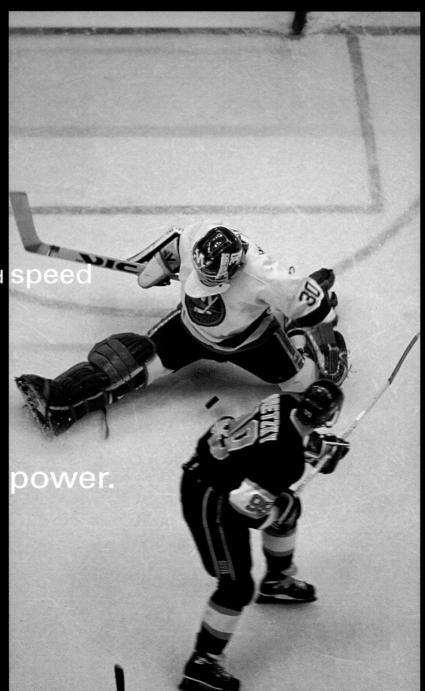

don't even think of a play, because they don't think that play is possible. And Gretzky makes that play.

So the first time I ever was on the ice with him was on the Oilers. I spent 10 years there watching him. Then I played against him, so I've seen both ends of it.

The first practice I had with him, you just start to realize how much better he was than what you thought. His whole game was better than what you realized, and it just gave you a greater appreciation. Things happen so much quicker on the ice than what you're seeing in the stands. And for him to be able to do all those things was amazing.

The season he scored 92 goals (in 1981-82), it seemed like he could score any time he pleased. Could he have scored even more goals that year? I think so. He had something like 203 points, so he set more up than he scored. There's a lot of those he probably could have scored.

But his shot is not a hard shot. It's just a very accurate shot. His release — sometimes it's quick, sometimes it's not quick. He can shoot against the flow really well. And he never really gives you a straight-on shot. It's always from an angle, or he's cutting across, or he's going against the flow and shooting back at you. He's never standing still, and there's always somebody standing in front of you. You never get a clear look at him. He uses his people well in front of you. The main thing is he's never stationary. That's why people have so much trouble hitting him. He moves around so much.

The thing about his shot is he shoots it better than it looks. And the toughest part about it is it's always in the right spot. For me, to be playing against him now, I have a bit of an advantage. It's not so much knowing what he's going to do, since I know how good he is.

In his **first season** with

the Rangers,

Wayne proved

he could still get **past**

the **defense** by notching

You don't take for granted that when it looks like he's out of the play, he's actually out of the play. You know you can't ever really relax if he's out there. If he gets behind the net and somebody shoots the puck wide, you know he's back there. And you don't take it for granted that the puck's gonna go wide.

Bernie Federko was the first center to really set up behind the net, but Wayne made it an art form. You can't give him time to set up back there. But if you run at him, it just creates more havoc with all the traffic. He'll turn it into chaos back there. He brings the defenseman with it. Then you've got guys all coming back toward the net. And if you've got players back at the net, the points are open. And he'll find them.

He's the best passer I've seen. It's his vision. He can find the open man, and then he always makes good passes. And he'll pass to a place, not a player. Somebody'll be headed to a place, and Wayne knows they can score from that spot, and that's where it goes.

In Edmonton, we had guys like Mark Messier and Paul Coffey and Jari Kurri and Glenn Anderson. We played a little run-and-gun hockey, which nobody else did back then. Our whole theory was a good offense is the best defense. It made it entertaining at times for me. We gave up some breakaways.

"You don't take for granted that when it looks like he's out of the play, he's actually out of the play."

From fun and games during **pregame** warm-ups to the serious **business** of hoisting trophies, Gretzky does it like no other.

I don't have enough years left for that.

He's still Wayne Gretzky. He can go as long as he wants to.

Grant Fuhr was the backbone of the Edmonton Oilers dynasty in the 1980s. With the Oilers, he won five Stanley Cup rings, played in six All-Star Games and won a Vezina Trophy (1987-88) as the best goalie in the NHL. Fuhr shared a Jennings Trophy in Buffalo after the 1993-94 season with Dominik Hasek for the lowest goals-against average by a team's goaltenders.

After playing together in Edmonton for seven years, Fuhr and Wayne Gretzky were reunited for a season in Los Angeles. They joined up a third time in St. Louis in the 1995-96 season, with Fuhr arriving first with an assist from Gretzky. Or more specifically, his wife, Janet, who recommended Fuhr to then Blues coach Mike Keenan.

"Mike asked me about Grant," Gretzky recalls, "but before I could say anything, my wife reached in, pushed me aside and said, 'Just sign him. And play him.' I guess he took this to heart.

"I've played with some great players, but he's the best athlete I've ever played with."

Tom Wheatley, who interviewed Grant Fuhr for this story, is a columnist for the St. Louis Post-Dispatch.

The Leader

I've always thought, and still think, the biggest thing about Wayne is his enthusiasm for the game. It's amazing. It's the same as it was his first year with the Oilers. And it's infectious. It seems to rub off on everybody. That was what made it so much fun to play with Wayne. There was always a good feeling that he had around him. There was always the aura he had about him in terms of what he could do for a team. He's a very strong presence. Somebody once said that it's a boost just to see his equipment hanging in the locker room. Wayne's presence gives a team confidence and respect. You never want to see one of your teammates out of the

BY MARK MESSIER

lineup, certainly not one of your leaders.

People talk about him being aware on the ice, but he's incredibly knowledgeable about the game off the ice. Wayne's a walking tote board. It's amazing. He knew more stats, not only on hockey, but on baseball and football. He's really into sports in general. He was always up to date about everything going on around the league. He was always well-informed.

Edmonton's dynasty centered on the presence of its captain, whose leadership even inspired stars such as Grant Fuhr.

When I played with him my last year in New York (1996-97) there were some changes from our days in Edmonton together. The biggest thing is you change as a person as the years go on, and you change as a professional, too. Your age dictates that you need more time to get ready for games, and you need more time to recuperate from them. As you get older your interests change. It's a natural progression, but his overall competitiveness hasn't changed one bit. He's a ruthless winner, and that's been well documented.

He has a real, pure instinct when it comes to winning. His enthusiasm, his competitiveness and will to win remain the same.

Everybody knows what a great player Wayne is as an individual, but part of that greatness is the way he can make other guys better, too. I think he'll be remembered for other things than what he's accomplished on his own. He's been a great team player, and guys who have played with him have benefited from that. Let's face it — it is a team game and you have to be able to tie into your teammates in order to be successful.

He's been able to elevate teammates to higher levels than perhaps they expected they could. That's one of the things that's added to what he is and made him a champion. Very few individuals have the ability to affect the whole team's game.

People see what a force Wayne can be during competition, but he's a strong

Wayne's move

to Los Angeles in 1988

paved the way

for expansion into **Anaheim**
and **San Jose.**

leader at all times. It's just that he maybe does it in a different way than some other people. He's always including everybody in everything. He has a strong personality. You don't want to mistake that. He gets his point across when he needs to.

When Wayne joined the Rangers last season it was very exciting for me. Every day last year was pretty enjoy-

able. I was really happy for Wayne to get a chance to come to New York and play in that competitive environment and see him with us in the playoffs doing what he does best. (The Rangers advanced to the Eastern Conference finals before falling to Philadelphia.)

For me, that was the most enjoyable thing about him coming to New York. I thought he could come in and play as well as he did (finishing fifth in scoring with 25 goals and 72 assists), but I don't know if everybody else did.

There were a lot of questions about how that would affect me, but my philosophy has been that whatever helps the team is best for everybody. From a leadership standpoint I think we just took up where we left off in Edmonton. We had a good fit. Our personalities

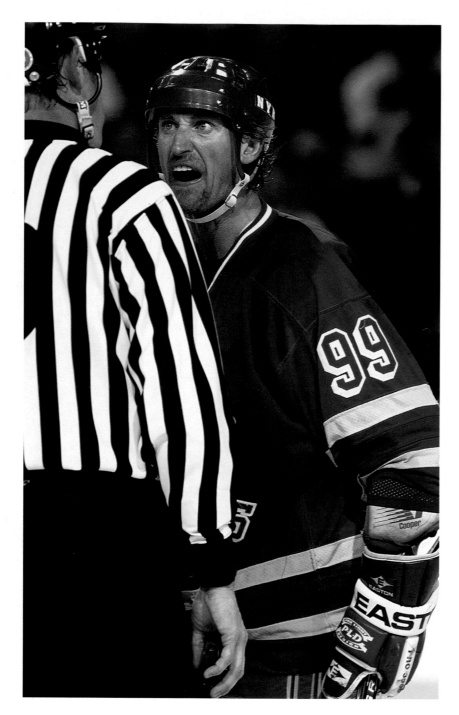

but it wasn't too long until we looked around the room and we had only ourselves to find our own way. There was myself, Kevin Lowe and Wayne — we were the core of the group — and (head coach) Glen Sather wanted it that way. We just kind of felt it out. Sure, we had some tough times, but I think our experience took us beyond the rough times and where we needed to be.

A s you get older you start to appreciate the relationships you've formed a lot more. I've played on some great teams over the years, but I've also met some pretty special people who have affected my life in a lot of ways, not only as a professional but from a personal standpoint, too.

Wayne is obviously one of those people.

There aren't many professional athletes with as strong a reputation for consummate leadership as Mark Messier. The Edmonton native has won two Hart Trophies, a Conn Smythe Trophy and has been a yearly fixture in the the NHL

were perfect for that kind of endeavor, and there never was a problem.

Wayne and I were put in a position when we first got to Edmonton that there were some experienced guys on the team and we just followed. They showed us around the league the first few years,

"A leader's got to
carry the air
of having

a team's
best interests
at heart,
all the time.
Wayne's like that."

— ex-Oilers teammate

Kevin Lowe

Preferring

to lead by example,

The Great One

strikes a **reassuring pose**
of **cool** determination.

All-Star Game. Messier was raised in a hockey environment — his father Doug was a career minor league defenseman — and turned pro at 17 to play in the World Hockey Association.

He was drafted the following year by the Edmonton Oilers, arrived the same year as the teenaged Wayne Gretzky and went·on to lead, with The Great One, the Oilers to four Stanley Cups in the mid-1980s.

The former teammates **will be reunited in the Hall of Fame.**

After Gretzky was traded to Los Angeles in the summer of 1988, Messier became captain of the Oilers and hasn't been without a "C" on his chest since. He was handed the captaincy upon being traded to the New York Rangers in 1991 and after signing as a free agent with the Vancouver Canucks in 1997.

Messier's pit-bull performance against Chicago in the conference final in 1990 en route to his fifth cup with Edmonton was one for the ages. So was his guarantee that the Rangers would win Game 6 and stave off elimination in the Eastern final against New Jersey in 1994. Messier scored three goals and added an assist in a 4-2 win, as the Rangers went on to claim their first Stanley Cup in 54 years.

Jim Jamieson, who interviewed Mark Messier for this story, covers the NHL for the Vancouver Province.

Second Period

BY WALTER GRETZKY

The Kid

When former National Hockey League player Paul Reinhart speaks at formal dinners these days, he talks about the day Grandma Gretzky went after him with a purse. Everyone thinks he's exaggerating, but his story is absolutely true. When Paul was playing for Kitchener (Ontario) and Wayne played for Brantford (Ontario), my mother was a true hockey fan. She attended many games at the Brantford arena, which at the time didn't have glass around the sideboards. In one league game, Paul checked Wayne into the boards, and then momentarily pinned him there, just like every defenseman does in every game played at every level of competition. My elderly mother (Mary)

it was clear at an early age that Wayne's drive to be successful was unique to say the least.

On Saturday afternoons in the winter, when friends would come to get him to go to the movie theater, he wouldn't go because he wanted to stay home and skate in the backyard. He would skate through pylons to practice his stick handling. He would shoot pucks by himself until it was too dark to see whether they hit the net or not. He would sometimes pay friends a nickel or a dime to stay around and play goal against him.

But what most people don't realize was that Wayne's love of sports went beyond hockey. He was in the Brantford Track and Field Club until he was 15. Given his reputation for endurance today, it's probably not surprising that he was a distance runner. He excelled at any race from 800 meters on up.

He also worshipped baseball and played for Brantford's travel teams until he was 15. When he was 11, a team in Chatham, Ontario, added him to the roster to pitch for the All-Canada

descended as quickly as she could from the stands to where Paul was holding Wayne against the boards. She started swinging her purse at Paul's head. It was a comical sight.

There weren't many dull moments for Wayne when he was a young player in his hometown of Brantford. He was like most kids growing up in Canada in the 1960s and 1970s: He watched TV, had a paper route, collected hockey cards and hung out with his friends. But

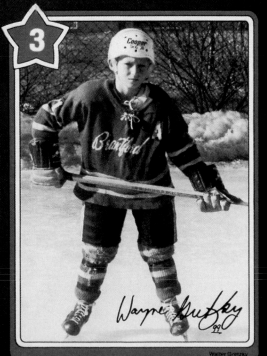

After wearing No. 9 for his Brantford Nadrofsky junior team, Wayne first donned his famous No. 99 for Sault Ste. Marie of the Ontario Minor Hockey Association. The Neilson's Gretzky trading card shows Wayne in his backyard rink.

He **quickly** became
a **popular** player,
even among **female** **fans.**

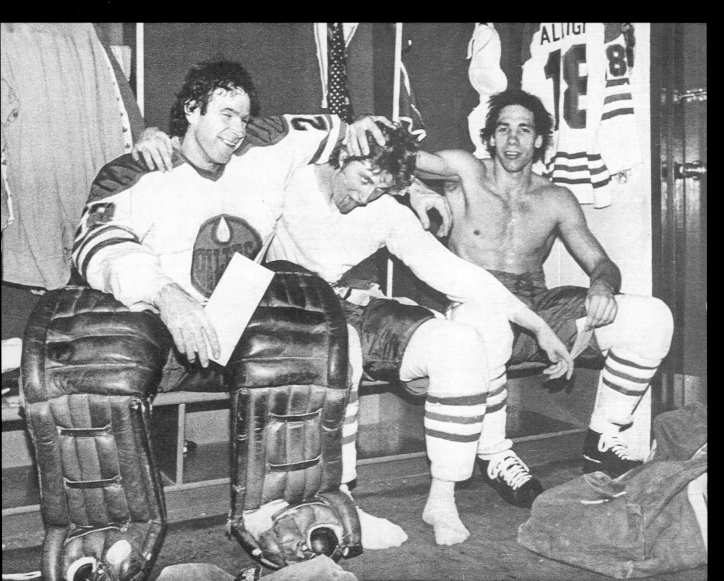

Championships in Saskatchewan. The Chatham team won that tournament. He was a pitcher and shortstop. As a young pitcher, he could strike out 15 to 19 players per game. He had a good fastball and a knuckleball that he used as a change-up.

We never knew whether Wayne was going to be big enough to be a pro player, but I always told him, "You may not be the biggest player, but you can always make yourself the quickest player and the smartest player. What you don't have to be is the toughest player."

It wasn't easy being Wayne Gretzky when he was a youngster. At every rink he went to in Canada, people had heard about him, especially after he scored 378 goals in one regular season for Brantford as an 11-year-old. My wife, Phyllis, and I tried to help Wayne deal with that pressure. We tried to instill in him a good value system, particularly a strong work ethic.

What some people don't know is that Wayne was an "A" student, because we always told him, "If you do well in school, that focus will help you be successful in sports." When he came home from school, he would always do his homework before he headed off to play hockey.

As supportive as we tried to be as a family, it was Wayne who had to overcome the pressure to perform on the ice. It was Wayne's inner drive that fueled him.

The play that describes how determined he was as a youngster happened at a tournament near Brantford when he had scored 49 goals in seven games over one weekend. He wanted his 50th goal, but it didn't look like he would get it after he was called for a three-minute tripping penalty — that's how long the penalties were then — with less than four minutes left in the seventh game.

The team was playing against a very good Little Caesars team out of Detroit. With less than a minute to go in the game, he exited the penalty box, picked up a loose puck at center ice, beat the defense and pulled the goaltender out of position with a beautiful deke and scored that 50th. That's how Wayne was as a youngster. When he put his mind to something, he accomplished it.

Everyone thinks I put a rink in the backyard so Wayne could develop into an NHL player. But let me tell you the real reason: self-preservation. I used to take him to the parks at night, and he would stay there for 2-1/2 hours, and I would freeze to death. One day, I came home and said to Phyllis, "This is ridiculous. I'm going to build a rink in the backyard so he can skate all he wants, and I can stay in the house where it's warm."

Wayne's drive seemed special to us. How many 10-year-olds shoot pucks off sheets of steel all summer to improve their accuracy?

But we never lost sight of the fact that Wayne was just a boy who could be frustrated, made uneasy and unnerved just like any other boy his age. That's

Walter had **a strong positive** influence on his son. **"I hope** I'm raising my kids the same **way that** my **parents raised** our family," says Wayne, who has **one** daughter, Paulina, and **two sons**, Ty and Trevor.

why one of my favorite stories involves the night the great Hall of Famer Gordie Howe, whom Wayne idolized, bailed him out of an embarrassing situation when Wayne was just 11 years old.

In recognition of his 378-goal season, Wayne was asked to sit at the head table, near Gordie, at the Great Men of Sport Dinner in Brantford. The master of ceremonies was simply supposed to introduce Wayne, and then Wayne was going to sit down. But that word never got to the emcee, who seemed to think Wayne was going to speak.

The emcee sat down, leaving poor Wayne standing embarrassed in front of a packed house at the Brantford Civic Center. Gordie realized what had happened and immediately went to the microphone and said, "You can sit down, because anyone who has scored 378 goals in one season doesn't have to say anything."

"When (Wayne) put his mind to something, he accomplished it."

When Wayne Gretzky was drawing international attention in the 1970s as a hockey prodigy and possibly the greatest youth player the world had ever seen, people would often ask Walter Gretzky how his kid was doing.

"Which one?" he would say. Walter and Phyllis Gretzky raised five children in Brantford, Ontario, and they were careful to make sure that they all received their share of attention.

"He was my hockey instructor," Wayne says of his father, whom he calls Wally. "He was also my lacrosse, baseball, basketball and cross country coach, not to mention my trainer and chauffeur. He is probably the smartest guy I know." Walter still lives in Brantford, and he still watches his son play every game. Only now, it's on the satellite dish.

Kevin Allen, who interviewed Walter Gretzky for this story, covers hockey for USA Today.

I've known Wayne Gretzky since I was maybe 6 years old. We grew up together in Brantford, Ontario, where we lived about a half-mile apart. All we did was play sports. We built a great friendship. It was a lot of fun growing up at that time in that community. Brantford was, for the time, a pretty good-sized town of about 60,000 people. But it had a small-town atmosphere. It was close-knit, and everyone pretty much knew each other. And everyone loved sports, especially the kids. Wayne and I, well, we took sports pretty seriously. We were real good friends and spent a lot of time together until he went to Sault Ste. Marie to play major junior and I went to Oshawa. We went our separate ways, but we still kept in touch. We'd play whatever was in season, but hockey and baseball were our favorites. We loved baseball — we really did. If he wasn't pitching and I wasn't playing shortstop, it was the other way around.

BY GREG STEFAN

The Phenom

As an 11-year-old,

Wayne Gretzky scored

an **incredible**

378 goals

in just **69 games**

We'd play every day in the summer. Wayne was pretty good at baseball, too. He could really play.

We played a lot of hockey, obviously. We took it pretty hard when we lost, even pick-up games. Wayne didn't like to lose at all. He still doesn't. You could see it in his eyes. He was, and still is, determined to win every time he goes on the ice. He's always been a special athlete in that sense. That determination and that attitude. Even in midgets he was determined to be the best player he could be.

Wayne was a pretty normal kid growing up. In the summer, we'd play from morning until night. There were a bunch of us from the neighborhood, and we'd get together and just play all day. We pushed each other to become the best players we could become.

Those games were intense. To this day, I really think those games, as well as anything we did athletically, helped us develop into pros. All of us were so competitive. Wayne and I hated to lose, so we'd do anything we could to win.

That competitiveness helped us reach the NHL.

We didn't care much about television in those days, except maybe *Hockey Night in Canada* (on Saturday nights). That was always on.

You could tell Wayne was a special athlete right off the bat. He was just a little better than the rest of us. He would be scoring 65, 70 goals a season and be able to make plays and passes nobody else could. He had a vision on the ice, even at that age, that no one else had. He has a gift. He's able to think a few plays ahead, and few players are able to do that. And he played with tremendous determination.

The strange part about it was, a lot of people, even after all Wayne accom-

"Everyone was waiting for Wayne to fall flat.

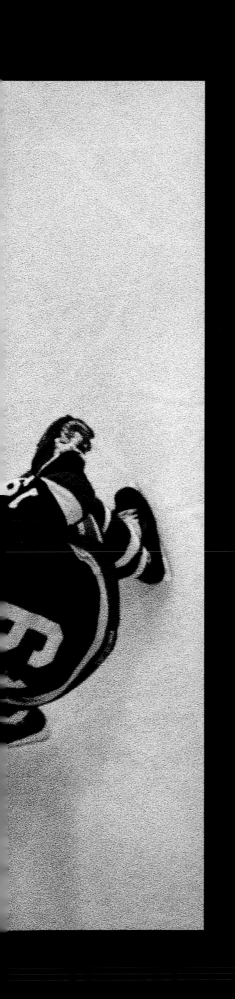

plished, expected him to fail. It always surprised me. Every time Wayne moved up a classification, they all thought he would fail. Whether it was peewee, bantam, midget, junior, whatever level it was, they would say Wayne wouldn't be big enough, fast enough, strong enough. I never could figure that out. He dominated every level. But everyone was waiting for Wayne to fall flat. It never happened.

Wayne always proved them wrong. Always. What Wayne has inside, only the great ones have. He has a special vision of the game, a special feel, that only players of that high caliber possess. It doesn't matter how strong, fast or physical you are.

During hockey season, there was always a certain amount of pressure on Wayne. Even when he was very young, many people knew about his talent and wanted to see him play.

There was the one time Gordie Howe came to Brantford and took that famous picture with the hockey stick poking Wayne's ears. That's about the time

people started to notice Wayne.

You'd think there'd be pressure, but Wayne handled it so well. I think Wayne grew up pretty quick because of the circumstances. He moved a couple of times to get away from Brantford to play hockey and develop his career. It really says a lot about him and his parents (Walter and Phyllis).

Early on, when Wayne was scoring all those goals, he was accused of selfish play. That was ridiculous. If there was a pass to be made Wayne would make it. He'd make the impossible look normal.

Selfish? That's just not true of Wayne. He had to score those goals because often times the other kids couldn't handle Wayne's passes. That's why Wayne had to keep it himself and shoot. That was the best way for our team to win.

But some of the parents didn't see it that way. They thought because Wayne was taking all the shots, keeping the puck, he was selfish and looking to pad his statistics. You know what, though? It was the parents who believed that. It wasn't the kids.

It was rough. Eventually Wayne had to move away to the Toronto area to play because of all the talk around town. It just wasn't fun. Let's face it, he didn't have a normal childhood.

His parents should be given a lot of credit for Wayne being the person he is, and for helping Wayne keep everything in perspective when he was young.

I think all those things happening early in his career actually toughened Wayne. People would come out to tournaments when we were 8- or 9-year-olds and might criticize him. He had to learn about that part of the game early and it definitely made a difference. He wasn't like most kids playing hockey. But Wayne learned to handle it.

Wayne has had a career like few people have ever had. People are always after his time, but Wayne always seems

Father Walter, mother Phyllis

and wife **Janet** have witnessed

most of Wayne's

brightest moments.

to give it to them. He's a gracious guy and does whatever is best for the game.

We usually find time in the summer to talk. We teach at a camp. That's always something I look forward to. He has a wonderful, beautiful family. I'm very happy for him. He's a fine example to young kids, young players coming up.

It was a lot of fun growing up in Brantford with Wayne. It was a special time.

"I think all those things happening early in his career actually **toughened** Wayne."

Greg Stefan has known Wayne Gretzky as long as anyone in hockey.

Stefan, who is exactly 16 days younger than Gretzky, played with Wayne on the 10-and-under Brantford Nadrofsky novice team. It was with a Nadrofsky team in 1972 that an 11-year-old Gretzky scored an eye-popping 378 goals in just 69 games.

That phenomenal year shoved a reluctant Gretzky into the hockey spotlight, where the attention was sometimes so unbearable that he would avoid autograph seekers by sending Stefan, adorned with a Gretzky jacket, out to sign for him. (Stefan sometimes signed the autographs as "Wayne Gretsky.")

At 14, the real Gretzky left his family and friends to play junior B hockey in Toronto. Amazingly, Stefan and Wayne had the talent to rise through the ranks of hockey and reach the National Hockey League.

Stefan played nine seasons in the NHL, all with the Detroit Red Wings. He played in 299 professional games, compiling a 115-127-30 record. He had five career shutouts and posted a 3.92 goals against average. When he suffered a strained left shoulder midway through the 1984-85 season, another Gretzky pal, Eddie Mio, was called up to spell him.

Stefan is now an assistant coach with the Plymouth (Mich.) Whalers in the Ontario Hockey League.

Ted Kulfan, who interviewed Greg Stefan for this story, covers the Whalers for The Detroit News.

6

The Rookie

BY EDDIE MIO

The first time I heard about Wayne Gretzky was during the summer back in my hometown of Windsor, Ontario. I was with some friends someplace, and someone asked me what it was going to be like playing with Wayne Gretzky. I wasn't sure who they were talking about. That was the first I had heard of the guy. I hadn't gotten much hockey news in the places I had played. I had never heard of Wayne. "Play with him?" I asked. "What's it going to be like for him to play with us?" After all, we were the pros. I had just never heard of him. But you have to remember where I was playing at the time. Places like Calgary, in Western Canada, while Wayne was out East in junior. I played in Birmingham, Ala., where hockey news was virtually nonexistent, and Indianapolis, where hockey was again not the major sport. So when people started talking about Wayne Gretzky, I really didn't know too much about him.

Gretzky's **first NHL assist** came against the Blackhawks when he set up Kevin Lowe for the score. It was the Edmonton club's first goal after joining the NHL.

You would never guess this was a young hockey superstar. He was just a young guy hanging out with people his own age.

You could tell Wayne had great hockey skills, even at 17 when he was playing with guys five or six years older. He was such a tremendous passer. He has great vision on the ice. He wasn't out of place playing professionally, even at his age. He always challenged himself; he was intent on becoming the best player he could become.

He turned out OK.

There were some guys who tested Wayne, trying to make runs at him, playing rough. But Wayne held up against whatever they came with. Or else he just got out of the way. He wouldn't get intimidated. He was strong mentally.

That first season (1978), Indy sold Wayne, myself and Peter Driscoll to Edmonton for something like $810,000, which at the time was the largest deal ever in sports. It was eight games into the season, so we knew something was up.

The deal came down to either Edmonton or Winnipeg, whoever had the more money. It turned out Edmonton came through with the better deal, so we were off to the Oilers, and the rest is history.

Edmonton was a great experience at the time. A lot of the players were about the same age. It was a great opportunity for a lot of talented, young hockey players to grow together. I was happy to be part of it with Wayne for a few years.

The friendship between Wayne and I had solidified itself through these years. I was five years older, but that actually worked out better because I became the big brother to Wayne he never had. Wayne was the oldest one in his family, and he carried all the responsibilities and burdens. This was an opportunity for him to let off some steam and have someone to listen to. I think he appreciated it, and it was a good experience for me.

Plus, having played professionally for a few years, I was able to offer whatever advice there was to give at the time. I helped him out whatever way I could.

That first year in Edmonton (1979, as an NHL team), I think we, the team and Wayne himself, all surprised some people around the league.

Wayne was unbelievable. He led the league in assists and points and won Most Valuable Player. He wasn't fazed by the league at all. He made an impact like few players have in their first seasons.

Going to Edmonton was another difficult transition for Wayne. It was similar to what happened in Indianapolis and wherever else Wayne had been. He was the main star, the person either the team or the league placed high expectations on. That's a lot of pressure to put on anybody.

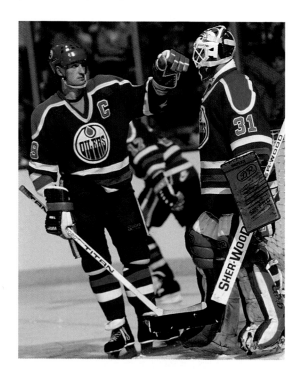

Wayne took some shots

early in his career

as defenders tried to rattle

the young star. But it soon

became apparent that at 6-feet,

170 pounds, Gretzky could play

with the big boys. At 19, he became

the youngest player in NHL history

to score 50 goals

in a season.

It was an honor to be the best man at Wayne's wedding to Janet. I think he picked me so he wouldn't create any controversy around his real good friends! He had a lot of them to choose from.

Still, it was very nice. It was a beautiful wedding, and Janet's a wonderful girl. They have a great family.

He's a great guy, and he's a true gentleman of the game.

Mio served as best man at Wayne's wedding to actress Janet Jones.

Few people have had the opportunity to see Wayne Gretzky mature like Eddie Mio.

Mio was Gretzky's teammate with Indianapolis and Edmonton in the WHA, then with the NHL's Oilers for two seasons. Unfortunately for Eddie, he missed out on Wayne and Edmonton's Stanley Cup runs as Mio was traded to the New York Rangers in 1981, three years before Gretzky won his first Stanley Cup.

With the Rangers, Mio led the team into the divisional finals round of the NHL playoffs twice, in 1981-82 and 1982-83. Both times, New York lost to the Islanders. Eddie was traded to Detroit in 1983 and went on to play three seasons with the Red Wings before retiring in 1986. Overall, Mio played seven seasons (1979-86), seeing action in 192 games. He had a 64-73-30 career record, with four shutouts while allowing a 4.06 goals against average.

Mio lives in the Detroit Area.

Ted Kulfan, who interviewed Eddie Mio for this story, covers the Plymouth (Mich.) Whalers in the Ontario Hockey League for The Detroit News.

Third Period

BY BRETT HULL

I would have to guess the first time I met Wayne was at the All-Star Game in Edmonton, my first All-Star Game (in 1989, Gretzky's first season with the Los Angeles Kings). For me, it was unbelievable. The legend of those Oilers at that time was unreal, and there I was in their dressing room. Wayne and Jari Kurri were playing pingpong, and Mark Messier was in there. And, of course, Wayne was the legend of the legends. If you can imagine me being a little intimidated, I didn't say much of anything. Honest to God, how often does that happen? You don't know what to expect when you meet a guy like that for the first time, and he was just the nicest guy in the world. Then when my

The Friend

agent, Bob Goodenow, took over the executive director job of the National Hockey League Players Association, he suggested that I go with Michael Barnett as my agent. Mike's been with Wayne since Day One. Wayne and I would get together on a couple of occasions. And then, all of a sudden, as my career started to take off, endorsements came and at times we did things together. And we just hit it off real good. It wasn't an immediate friendship thing. He's a quiet guy. He's not like me at all, which is why we probably get along so well together.

You're gonna know if I like you right off the bat. He's such a quiet guy, you don't really know how you stand with him right away. It seemed like the more time we spent together, though, the more fun we had.

We both worked for Easton and we had to do photo shoots (for the sporting goods company). We both worked for Upper Deck, and one year (the card company) sent us to San Diego to the baseball All-Star Game to do a photo shoot, and we spent the weekend there and went golfing. As we kind of got closer, we belonged to the Sherwood Country Club in L.A. He came up to my golf tournament (in Duluth, Minn.), and I went up to his softball tournament in Brantford, Ontario. That may have been a couple of the most enjoyable days I've ever had. When he puts something on, boy, he puts something on first class.

When he considers you a friend, you're definitely in good company. He's the type of guy who loves to do things. We just decided one year to play golf in Scotland. And he and I went with Marty McSorley and five of Wayne's other buddies from L.A. Wayne's such a fun person to be with. He has an unbelievably good sense of humor. He's one of the most fun guys to go golfing with.

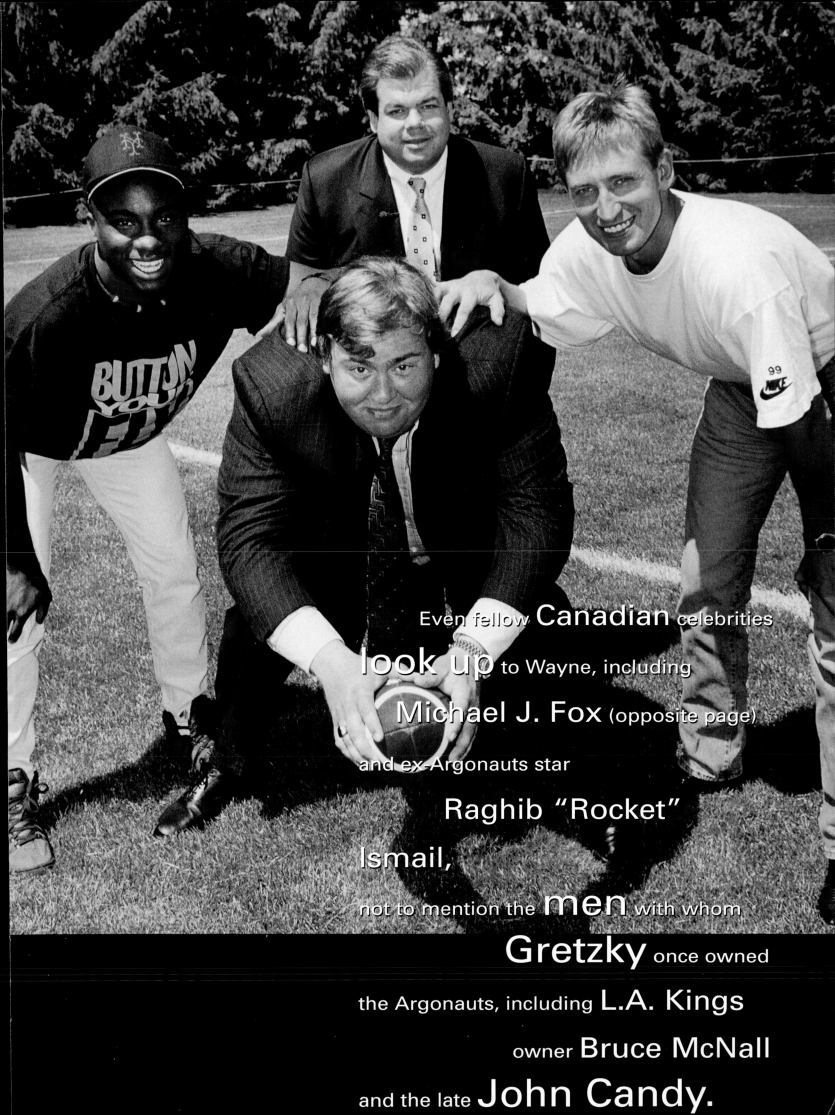

Even fellow **Canadian** celebrities **look up** to Wayne, including **Michael J. Fox** (opposite page) and ex-Argonauts star **Raghib "Rocket" Ismail,** not to mention the **men** with whom **Gretzky** once owned the Argonauts, including L.A. Kings owner **Bruce McNall** and the late **John Candy.**

He likes to needle you, but he likes to needle himself. If I have to go to L.A. to do something, the first thing he says is, "You're staying at my house." His family is so great to be with, Janet and the kids, and he's an unbelievable family man. Janet is super, super nice, and she has a great sense of humor, too. She was in that *Police Academy* movie, and I tell you what, she'd be a great comic actress.

They start kidding, and they give it back and forth to each other. She's like me. She tells it like it is. And Wayne's like, "Janet, come on!" His favorite line to me is, "Hullie, I love you because you say everything I want to say."

He loves the game, too. So do I, but he tries to make the game great in a different way than I do. I try to open everybody's eyes. He's the ambassador. He's so inundated in a town like St. Louis. Everybody recognizes him when he goes out. That's why New York and L.A. are so perfect for him. People say to me, "How do you ever go out in St. Louis?"

But he's a hundred times more inundated than I am. He can get lost in the big cities because those people are so used to seeing movie stars and celebrities. Sometimes they might recognize him and say hi, but sometimes they don't even say anything. A lot of times people in New York and L.A. don't even recognize him. He can put a hat on and coat, and he looks like a normal Joe.

The great thing is that he acts like a normal Joe. You've got that preconceived notion of what the guy would be, and then you meet him and say, "This can't be Wayne Gretzky. He's way too down to earth."

I don't care if I get five Stanley Cups, the best 31 games of my career were here

The **Blues'** alternate **captain gladly** gave up the 'A' on his sweater during **spring 1996** when he learned he would be **skating alongside** the **Babe Ruth of hockey.**

Brett led the NHL in goals scored three times and claimed regular season MVP honors in 1991, but his career highlight was playing 31 games with The Great One.

Hull offered to give his 'A' as alternate captain to Shayne Corson, then the Blues' captain, who was handing his 'C' to Gretzky. "You can have my 'A,' " Hull told Corson. "I don't care. I just want to get him here. I've played with some of the worst centers in the game, and now I get to play with the best one."

The jokes fly when wife Janet and Brett take aim at Wayne.

Gretzky, who included Hull on his tour of Europe during the labor stoppage in 1994, is a longtime admirer of his friend's skills. The droll Gretzky wit was at work after their first practice together under Mike Keenan. "That No. 16 has potential," said Gretzky. "I'm going to tell Mike we should keep him."

Tom Wheatley, who interviewed Brett Hull for this story, is a columnist for the St. Louis Post-Dispatch.

The Idol

I remember the first time I saw Wayne Gretzky play live, in Vancouver. I must have been 10 or 11, and he was my idol. He was with Edmonton, and the fans were booing every time he touched the puck. I was the only one cheering. I got a lot of dirty looks. Growing up, the only games we really got were *Hockey Night in Canada*. He'd be on Saturday night a lot, and then he'd be in Vancouver three times a year. I still remember the day he was traded. I was riding home from

BY PAUL KARIYA

Wayne always finds time for questions from the media

that swarms around him after games.

school in the car with my mom, and she told me he was going to be traded to Los Angeles.

I didn't believe her. For me, at that time, I didn't know the business side. All I knew was he won championships. I thought he would never go anywhere. But I quickly turned into a Los Angeles Kings fan.

I mean, he was the best player in the world. It was the style of game he played. I could relate to him.

He's not a big guy. He played a style that is very cerebral, and he always had great skills. He was a player that I could more easily emulate than a Mark Messier or a Mario Lemieux.

When I was 14 or 15, I got my first Gretzky tape and started watching it. That creativity . . . never the same thing twice. He was always creating new

moves. And it was the way he was always unselfish that had a lot of appeal for me.

Growing up, I always played with older guys, and I figured out real early that you could get on their good side by setting them up and moving the puck to them.

You know, he always had more assists than goals, even when he was scoring 70, 80, even 92 goals that one year (1981-82, when he had 120 assists).

The first time I met him, I was visiting Boston University when I was being recruited before I decided to go to Maine. We went to a Bruins game, and he happened to be in town. I got a stick after the game, and I still have it.

It was always a great honor when people compared me to him, even though he should be put on a pedestal with no one else even close. But when you're compared to your idol and someone you respect, that's special. When I was younger, I was just thrilled by being compared to him. Now as I'm

"It was **always a great honor**

when people compared **me** to him,

even though he should be

put on a **pedestal**

with **no one** else even close."

Gretzky, far left, lent a hand to linemates Mark Messier, center, and Mario Lemieux, right, at the 1987 Canada Cup.

getting older, I'm trying to create my own identity.

One of the reasons I played in the Olympics in 1994 was because it made an impression on me that he said the one thing he always wanted to do was play in the Olympics. Coming from him, someone who had done everything, that put a lot more emphasis for me on how lucky I was to have the chance to play. If things hadn't changed and I didn't play when I did, I would never have had that chance.

I still admire the way he's handled himself with everything from an early age. The media, the fans — he's had a level of attention I can't even imagine.

In seven-plus **seasons with the Kings,** Gretzky amassed a **whopping** 918 points.

With everything outside of hockey, as well as what he does on the ice, he's kept such a clean image. Everything he's done has been so professional, with so much class.

When you're in the public eye at that level, everybody looks to knock you off that pedestal, but nobody's been able to do it.

After three years in the NHL, I have an even greater appreciation of the situation he's been in. What he's gone through . . . I've had nothing compared to that level of attention. And there are definitely times when you're overwhelmed. After practice, sometimes you just want to go home, but the media and fans are always there.

Without him, though, we probably wouldn't have a team in Anaheim. That can also be said in San Jose. People forget now, but until he came to Los Angeles, hockey was going nowhere in California. He created two more teams, not directly, but indirectly.

He's had such a profound effect on the game of hockey.

Paul Kariya was 4 years old when Wayne Gretzky made his NHL debut in 1978 and was a 14-year-old fan for life when Wayne was traded to the Los Angeles Kings 10 years later.

Kariya since has developed a following of his own. After just three NHL seasons, he became

the Anaheim Mighty Ducks' all-time leader in goals, assists, points and shots.

The left winger was voted a finalist for the Calder Memorial Trophy for the NHL's most outstanding rookie following his debut in 1994-95. In that season, Paul set the Mighty Ducks record for rookie points with 39, 65 less than Gretzky had during his first year in the NHL.

During the next two seasons, Kariya emerged as one of the league's best young players and became the latest in a long line of challengers to Gretzky's "The Great One" moniker. He scored 108 points in 1995-96 and followed that with 99 points the next season.

"Everything he's done has been so professional, with so much class."

Kariya, whose father is Japanese, played for the University of Maine from 1992 to '94 before joining Team Canada for the 1994 Olympics, during which he scored seven points to lead the silver medal-winning team.

Robyn Norwood, who interviewed Paul Kariya for this story, covers hockey for The Los Angeles Times.

The Patriot

BY MIKE KEENAN

I'll never forget the first day I coached Wayne Gretzky. It was back in the fall of 1987, and I was coaching Team Canada in the Canada Cup. It was the first weekend of August and we were just starting training camp in Montreal. I'll never forget what happened that day. There were distractions everywhere. All the players were reporting to camp, there were all kinds of organizers around, and there had to be at least 50 media people surrounding Wayne as he was making his way to the ice. He was very gracious and cordial to the media, but you could tell he wanted to move on. I was standing at center ice at the time watching this, taking it all in. He slowly moved towards the ice, but you could tell he wanted to make sure he was on the ice for practice on time. When his skates finally touched the ice, his eyes lit up like saucers. It was amazing.

Being on the ice is where he found his peace. It's where he wanted to be. It was the one domain where he was just free to play hockey, away from everything else, where he was in control. That day Wayne showed why he is one of the greatest players ever in the game, by the way he handled himself off the ice and the magic feeling when he stepped on it.

Gretzky led **Team Canada** to Canada Cup **titles** in **1984, 1987 and 1991** and was **the team's captain** in the **1996 World Cup** of Hockey.

He showed us great leadership throughout the tournament, but that day we knew we had a leader.

And he never let us down. We went on to win the tournament, which will probably be remembered as one of the greatest international series ever (Canada's thrilling two-games-to-one finals win over the Soviet Union), and Wayne's performance (21 points in nine games) will not soon be forgotten, either.

An interesting process happened in that Canada Cup. Wayne was at a point in his career where he still wanted to be the very best, but at the same time there was a young fellow by the name of Mario Lemieux coming on strong, and Wayne knew it. Wayne did something then that was unbelievable from a coach's perspective. He pretty well tried to teach Mario everything he knew about the game. He did it first because he was so unselfish and he wanted Team Canada to be strong, and second because he wanted to be pushed.

So, Wayne basically said, "There you are Mario, here's everything I know, but I'm still going to be the best." As it turned out, he helped push Mario to another level, but he also pushed himself in the process.

Obviously, Wayne has had a lot of success for his country in international

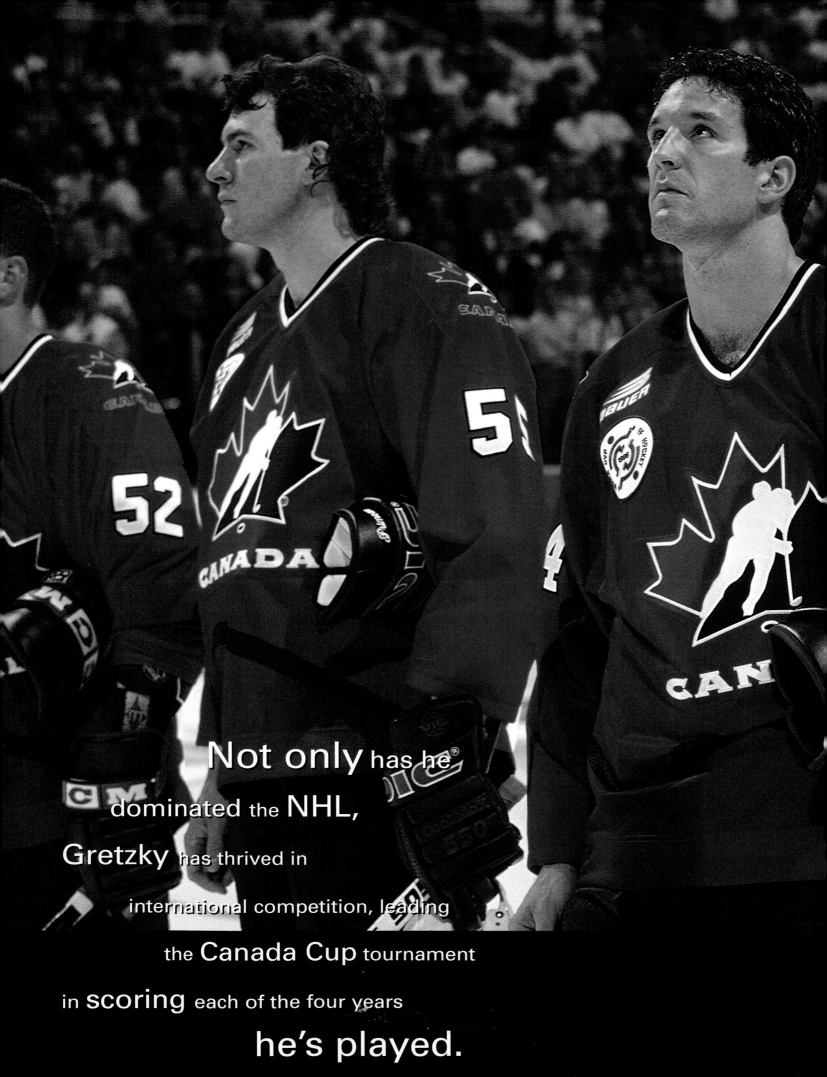

Not only has he® dominated the NHL, **Gretzky** has thrived in international competition, leading the **Canada Cup** tournament in **scoring** each of the four years **he's played.**

competition, and he has certainly made his mark in the NHL, but what he means to Canadians goes far beyond wins and losses in big tournaments.

He is a national treasure.

Canadians take their hockey seriously. They want to be the best, and Gretzky has not only allowed them to boast having produced one of the greatest players ever, but he has led the nation on the ice.

Canadians are very proud of the fact that Wayne comes from Canada and has become known around the world. He has made us all feel proud. As a country, we don't stick our collective chests out nearly enough, and when we do, it's usually related to something that has happened in relation to hockey.

And Wayne has often had a hand in it.

I think what really makes him great is his intelligence and his perception. Not very much gets by him on a daily basis, on the ice and around the league.

In many ways he is more of an artist. He leads with his skills and his innate ability to play the game. I think people realize that players of his caliber only come along once every so often, and when you get a chance to watch him play, you have to appreciate it, because one day he will no longer be playing.

But I can honestly say that of all the players I coached — and I had some wonderful players with guys like Rick Tocchet — I don't think I coached anyone who had a bigger heart than Wayne.

He's a small man in physical stature, but when we had to have things done in the Canada Cup — and this is another reason why he is so highly regarded by Canadians — he would push himself so hard he would be at the point of exhaustion.

You could give him any amount of

"He has certainly made his mark in the NHL, but what he means to Canadians goes far beyond wins and losses . . . He is a national treasure."

During their Team Canada
time together, Gretzky tutored
Lemieux on the subtle
nuances of the game.

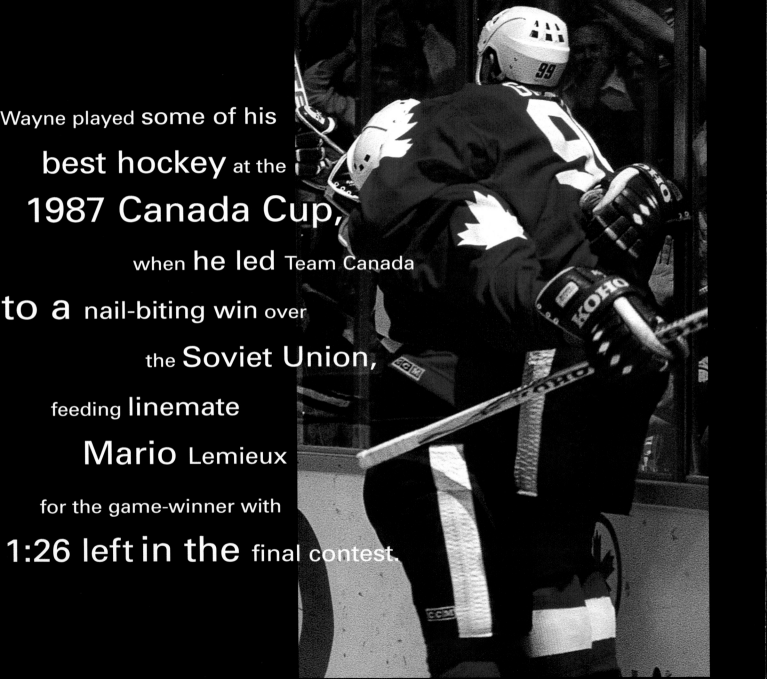

Wayne played some of his best hockey at the 1987 Canada Cup, when he led Team Canada to a nail-biting win over the Soviet Union, feeding linemate Mario Lemieux for the game-winner with 1:26 left in the final contest.

responsibility, any amount of ice time, and he would accept it and drive himself to play harder and better. He always put a huge premium on winning, and he had a drive that separated him from the rest.

He has been a great ambassador for the game, sacrificing a lot of time to help the game. And he never said no to representing his country. That's something that has endeared him to the Canadian fans, as well.

I t's like that first day of training in 1987. There he was surrounded by all those media people — you could see he was getting a little frustrated — but he remained cordial because he knew that was an important part of his job, and he knew that he was the leader of his country's team.

But you could just tell that he would have preferred to say (politely), "Hey, guys, I'm going to play hockey." But when he got on that ice, look out. . . .

Mike Keenan has been a successful, and well-traveled, coach in the NHL since 1984, working in Philadelphia, in Chicago, in New York with the Rangers and in St. Louis. Early in the 1997-98 season, he made his fifth NHL stop, taking over in November in Vancouver. He has coached teams to the Stanley Cup finals four times and led the Rangers to their first championship in 54 years in 1994. He has finished with the best regular season record in the NHL three times with three different teams.

He twice coached Gretzky and Team Canada to victory in Canada Cup competitions. But Keenan remembers being beaten by Gretzky-led teams as well. His Flyers teams were twice beaten by Gretzky and the Oilers in the 1985 and 1987 Stanley Cup finals. As coach and general manager in St. Louis, he traded for Gretzky in 1996.

Scott Morrison, who interviewed Mike Keenan for this story, is the sports editor of The Toronto Sun.

Overtime

The Legacy

I never played against Wayne Gretzky. I missed both Gordie Howe and Gretzky. I just wish, and the same with Mario Lemieux, that I knew what it felt like to play against them. Chances are, you'd have the same lack of results as everybody else, but you'd like to find out. Gretzky could and can do so many things. To me, that's the real difference between Gretzky and the rest. Gretzky was the first great forward whose way of playing was to make everybody around him better, not for everyone else around him to make him better.

BY KEN DRYDEN

After receiving a Gordie Howe No. 9 sweater for a Christmas present at an early age, Wayne Gretzky considered Howe his idol. The two have since become friends.

The style of play was always where you had to get Bobby Hull the puck, or you had to get Frank Mahovlich the puck, or Rocket Richard. Their style of game was to get it to them on the fly, and they'd make the play. The other four people on the ice were basically there to set up this great player.

Gretzky's style was always to force his teammates to be better. He'd give them the puck, but they had to skate in order to get to the puck, and they had to learn to handle the puck. Plus, they had to learn how to pass the puck to give it back to him. What was happening was that the focal point was dispersed. Where do you focus your attention? On him or the other people?

The challenge is you have to stop this five-man attack, and not just a one-man attack. And that's what strikes fear into the heart of any defenseman or goalie — not knowing exactly where to put your attention or effort.

Gretzky knows this. I remember talking to him once, and he said, "Look at me. I'm 175 pounds. I can't run people over. I can't insist on this piece of ice being mine if somebody else is there. What I have to do is be where other people aren't. If I am where other people are, I'm going to be neutralized."

He can't be Bobby Hull. But here's what he can be: He'll go with every punch, go to the open space, and create the open space not by carrying the puck but by passing it. Once he has the space, well, then he can handle it.

I think Gretzky's love of the game

Part of **Gretzky's greatness** comes from his respect for the game and legends such as **Gordie Howe.** "They often tell you," Wayne remarks, **"when you meet your heroes** and idols, you walk away saying, 'Well, they're not that nice, or just OK.' But Gordie, **he was bigger and better** than I ever imagined."

and the image of that sport, so Gretzky's impact in that way is very large.

I don't rank players (in the context of) all time. I rank players by generation — whether they were the best of their time. He's the best of his time.

To me there are two categories: whether you're the best of your time and whether you're an important player. There are a lot of players who may be very successful or very good but they don't add anything to the game. They don't leave a legacy behind. The game carries on in the same way without them.

Gretzky offers a style of game that's different. In many ways, he was the acceptable face of the European style in the NHL. Without a Canadian playing that kind of style, it would have been that much longer before people came to it.

Off the ice, as others were more willing to notice hockey, he was the one they noticed, and how appropriate that was, too.

The times have a way of making a

really comes across. There's no coach, teacher or parent who can get you to do things you ultimately don't want to do. The great player, the great performer or the great musician is somebody who spends time at what they're doing. It's time between games, between lessons, where the greatness in anything is made. It's fool-around time, being-by-yourself time. Take the lessons you've learned and create something new. You only do that if you love it. You don't spend the extra time if you don't love it.

The point often made about hockey players is that they're still the most normal and most accessible of all the professional athletes, and Gretzky is the most accessible and normal of the great superstars. People think this guy isn't like their neighbors, but he almost could be. The greatest player of any sport is always the face of that sport

Wayne broke one Gordie Howe record

with **goal No. 802,** top photo,

on March 23, 1994. Five years earlier, on

Oct. 15, **Wayne's goal** had given

him his **1,851st career**

point, bottom photo,

breaking Howe's hallowed record.

player unique. The actual player can be duplicated, but the circumstances change so the copy doesn't have the same results.

There will be others who will be heavily influenced by Gretzky. A far greater legacy than being unique and having no coattails is to be unique in your time and have coattails for other generations.

Gretzky, I think, will have very long coattails.

"Gretzky was the first great forward

whose way of playing was to make everybody around him better."

Ken Dryden, president and general manager of the Toronto Maple Leafs, got his first glimpse of Gretzky's talent during the 1973-74 season when he was doing television broadcasts for the Toronto Toros of the World Hockey Association.

Gretzky participated in a promotion where peewee hockey players were given the oportunity to attempt a penalty shot against backup goalie Les Binkley. Dryden remembers that the young phenom, despite an impressive move, failed to score on Binkley.

"And Gretzky, as he was skating away, slammed his stick down on the ice," Dryden says. "That's what I remember. A 12-year-old kid playing against a good, experienced professional goaltender comes in on goal, doesn't score, and he's upset. That was the first time I saw Gretzky."

Dryden has had plenty of opportunities to view and write about The Great One since that memorable day. A lawyer and member of the Hockey Hall of Fame's class of 1983, Dryden wrote two acclaimed books about hockey, The Game *and* Home Game. *The former goaltender for the Montreal Canadiens also has worked as a color commentator for ABC-TV at the Winter Olympics in 1980, '84 and '88.*

Damien Cox, who interviewed Ken Dryden for this story, covers the NHL for the Toronto Star.

photo credits